Francis Frith's
Villages of Devon

Malmsmead, The Ford, Lorna Doone's Farm c1960 M14023

Photographic Memories

Francis Frith's
Villages of Devon

Martin Dunning

FRITH
BOOK Co

First published in the United Kingdom in 2001 by
Frith Book Company Ltd

Paperback Edition 2001
ISBN 1-85937-293-7

Hardback Edition 2001
ISBN 1-85937-444-1

British Library Cataloguing in Publication Data

Francis Frith's Villages of Devon
Martin Dunning

Frith Book Company Ltd
Frith's Barn, Teffont,
Salisbury, Wiltshire SP3 5QP
Tel: +44 (0) 1722 716 376
Email: info@frithbook.co.uk
www.frithbook.co.uk

Printed and bound in Great Britain

Front Cover: Bere Alston, The Village 1898 42262

AS WITH ANY HISTORICAL DATABASE THE FRITH ARCHIVE IS CONSTANTLY BEING CORRECTED AND IMPROVED
AND THE PUBLISHERS WOULD WELCOME INFORMATION ON OMISSIONS OR INACCURACIES

Contents

Francis Frith: *Victorian Pioneer*

FRANCIS FRITH, Victorian founder of the world-famous photographic archive, was a complex and multi-talented man. A devout Quaker and a highly successful Victorian businessman, he was both philosophic by nature and pioneering in outlook.

By 1855 Francis Frith had already established a wholesale grocery business in Liverpool, and sold it for the astonishing sum of £200,000, which is the equivalent today of over £15,000,000. Now a multi-millionaire, he was able to indulge his passion for travel. As a child he had pored over travel books written by early explorers, and his fancy and imagination had been stirred by family holidays to the sublime mountain regions of Wales and Scotland. 'What a land of spirit-stirring and enriching scenes and places!' he had written. He was to return to these scenes of grandeur in later years to 'recapture the thousands of vivid and tender memories', but with a different purpose. Now in his thirties, and captivated by the new science of photography, Frith set out on a series of pioneering journeys to the Nile regions that occupied him from 1856 until 1860.

Intrigue and Adventure

He took with him on his travels a specially-designed wicker carriage that acted as both dark-room and sleeping chamber. These far-flung journeys were packed with intrigue and adventure. In his life story, written when he was sixty-three, Frith tells of being held captive by bandits, and of fighting 'an awful midnight battle to the very point of surrender with a deadly pack of hungry, wild dogs'. Sporting flowing Arab costume, Frith arrived at Akaba by camel seventy years before Lawrence, where he encountered 'desert princes and rival sheikhs, blazing with jewel-hilted swords'.

During these extraordinary adventures he was assiduously exploring the desert regions bordering the Nile and patiently recording the antiquities and peoples with his camera. He was the first photographer to venture beyond the sixth cataract. Africa was still the mysterious 'Dark Continent', and Stanley and Livingstone's historic meeting was a decade into the future. The conditions for picture taking confound belief. He laboured for hours in his wicker dark-room in the sweltering heat of the desert, while the volatile chemicals fizzed dangerously in their trays. Often he was forced to work in remote tombs and caves where conditions were cooler. Back in London he exhibited his photographs and was 'rapturously cheered' by members of the Royal Society. His reputation as a

photographer was made overnight. An eminent modern historian has likened their impact on the population of the time to that on our own generation of the first photographs taken on the surface of the moon.

Venture of a Life-Time

Characteristically, Frith quickly spotted the opportunity to create a new business as a specialist publisher of photographs. He lived in an era of immense and sometimes violent change. For the poor in the early part of Victoria's reign work was a drudge and the hours long, and people had precious little free time to enjoy themselves. Most had no transport other than a cart or gig at their disposal, and had not travelled far beyond the boundaries of their own town or village. However,

by the 1870s, the railways had threaded their way across the country, and Bank Holidays and half-day Saturdays had been made obligatory by Act of Parliament. All of a sudden the ordinary working man and his family were able to enjoy days out and see a little more of the world.

With characteristic business acumen, Francis Frith foresaw that these new tourists would enjoy having souvenirs to commemorate their days out. In 1860 he married Mary Ann Rosling and set out with the intention of photographing every city, town and village in Britain. For the next thirty years he travelled the country by train and by pony and trap, producing fine photographs of seaside resorts and beauty spots that were keenly bought by millions of Victorians. These prints were painstakingly pasted into family albums and pored over during the dark nights of winter, rekindling precious memories of summer excursions.

The Rise of Frith & Co

Frith's studio was soon supplying retail shops all over the country. To meet the demand he gathered about him a small team of photographers, and published the work of independent artist-photographers of the calibre of Roger Fenton and Francis Bedford. In order to gain some understanding of the scale of Frith's business one only has to look at the catalogue issued by Frith & Co in 1886: it runs to some 670 pages, listing not only many thousands of views of the British Isles but also many photographs of most European countries, and China, Japan, the USA and Canada – note the sample page shown above from the hand-written *Frith & Co* ledgers detailing pictures taken. By 1890 Frith had created the greatest specialist photographic publishing company in the world,

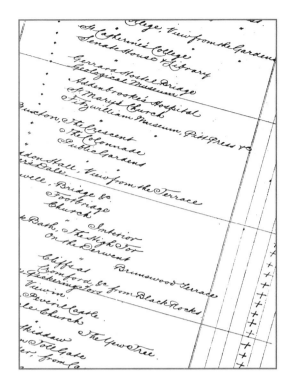

with over 2,000 outlets – more than the combined number that Boots and WH Smith have today! The picture on the right shows the *Frith & Co* display board at Ingleton in the Yorkshire Dales. Beautifully constructed with mahogany frame and gilt inserts, it could display up to a dozen local scenes.

Postcard Bonanza

The ever-popular holiday postcard we know today took many years to develop. In 1870 the Post Office issued the first plain cards, with a pre-printed stamp on one face. In 1894 they allowed other publishers' cards to be sent through the mail with an attached adhesive halfpenny stamp. Demand grew rapidly, and in 1895 a new size of postcard was permitted called the court card, but there was little room for illustration. In 1899, a year after

Frith's death, a new card measuring 5.5 x 3.5 inches became the standard format, but it was not until 1902 that the divided back came into being, with address and message on one face and a full-size illustration on the other. *Frith & Co* were in the vanguard of postcard development, and Frith's sons Eustace and Cyril continued their father's monumental task, expanding the number of views offered to the public and recording more and more places in Britain, as the coasts and countryside were opened up to mass travel.

Francis Frith died in 1898 at his villa in Cannes, his great project still growing. The archive he created continued in business for another seventy years. By 1970 it contained over a third of a million pictures of 7,000 cities, towns and villages. The massive photographic record Frith has left to us stands as a living monument to a special and very remarkable man.

Frith's Archive: *A Unique Legacy*

FRANCIS FRITH'S legacy to us today is of immense significance and value, for the magnificent archive of evocative photographs he created provides a unique record of change in 7,000 cities, towns and villages throughout Britain over a century and more. Frith and his fellow studio photographers revisited locations many times down the years to update their views, compiling for us an enthralling and colourful pageant of British life and character.

We tend to think of Frith's sepia views of Britain as nostalgic, for most of us use them to conjure up memories of places in our own lives with which we have family associations. It often makes us forget that to Francis Frith they were records of daily life as it was actually being lived in the cities, towns and villages of his day. The Victorian age was one of great and often bewildering change for ordinary people, and though the pictures evoke an impression of slower times, life was as busy and hectic as it is today.

We are fortunate that Frith was a photographer of the people, dedicated to recording the minutiae of everyday life. For it is this sheer wealth of visual data, the painstaking chronicle of changes in dress, transport, street layouts, buildings, housing, engineering and landscape that captivates us so much today. His remarkable images offer us a powerful link with the past and with the lives of our ancestors.

Today's Technology

Computers have now made it possible for Frith's many thousands of images to be accessed almost instantly. In the Frith archive today, each photograph is carefully 'digitised' then stored on a CD Rom. Frith archivists can locate a single photograph amongst thousands within seconds. Views can be catalogued and sorted under a variety of categories of place and content to the immediate benefit of researchers.

Inexpensive reference prints can be created for them at the touch of a mouse button, and a wide range of books and other printed materials assembled and published for a wider, more general readership - in the next twelve months over a hundred Frith local history titles will be published! The day-to-day workings of the archive are very different from how they were in Francis Frith's time: imagine the herculean task of sorting through eleven tons of glass negatives as Frith had to do to locate a particular sequence of pictures! Yet

See Frith at www. frithbook.co.uk

the archive still prides itself on maintaining the same high standards of excellence laid down by Francis Frith, including the painstaking cataloguing and indexing of every view.

It is curious to reflect on how the internet now allows researchers in America and elsewhere greater instant access to the archive than Frith himself ever enjoyed. Many thousands of individual views can be called up on screen within seconds on one of the Frith internet sites, enabling people living continents away to revisit the streets of their ancestral home town, or view places in Britain where they have enjoyed holidays. Many overseas researchers welcome the chance to view special theme selections, such as transport, sports, costume and ancient monuments.

We are certain that Francis Frith would have heartily approved of these modern developments in imaging techniques, for he himself was always working at the very limits of Victorian photographic technology.

The Value of the Archive Today

Because of the benefits brought by the computer, Frith's images are increasingly studied by social historians, by researchers into genealogy and ancestory, by architects, town planners, and by teachers and schoolchildren involved in local history projects.

In addition, the archive offers every one of us an opportunity to examine the places where we and our families have lived and worked down the years. Highly successful in Frith's own era, the archive is now, a century and more on, entering a new phase of popularity.

The Past in Tune with the Future

Historians consider the Francis Frith Collection to be of prime national importance. It is the only archive of its kind remaining in private ownership and has been valued at a million pounds. However, this figure is now rapidly increasing as digital technology enables more and more people around the world to enjoy its benefits.

Francis Frith's archive is now housed in an historic timber barn in the beautiful village of Teffont in Wiltshire. Its founder would not recognize the archive office as it is today. In place of the many thousands of dusty boxes containing glass plate negatives and an all-pervading odour of photographic chemicals, there are now ranks of computer screens. He would be amazed to watch his images travelling round the world at unimaginable speeds through network and internet lines.

The archive's future is both bright and exciting. Francis Frith, with his unshakeable belief in making photographs available to the greatest number of people, would undoubtedly approve of what is being done today with his lifetime's work. His photographs, depicting our shared past, are now bringing pleasure and enlightenment to millions around the world a century and more after his death.

Villages of Devon
An Introduction

FOR MOST PEOPLE, the phrase 'Devon village' will conjure up the steep, cobbled streets of Clovelly, or perhaps the thatched roofs of Lustleigh nestling in a fold of the Dartmoor landscape. Both villages have a chocolate-box quality about them; they have deservedly adorned postcards and tourist information leaflets by the million, but to label them as 'typical' Devon villages is misleading, for they represent only one small aspect of the diversity the county has to offer.

Devon is a vast county. It covers 2,588 square miles, stretching 75 miles from Foreland Point in the north to Prawle Point on the English Channel, and running east-west an almost equal distance from the Atlantic coast near Morwenstow to the Dorset border east of the valley of the River Axe. It has 9,000 miles of road and a population of over a million, of whom nearly half live in Plymouth, Exeter and Torbay. A further 300,000 live in towns. This leaves perhaps 200,000 spread across the huge rural portion of the county in villages ranging from the truly tiny, such as Harford, which has around 80 souls, to places such as Kingskerswell, which, although a village when Frith and his descendants photographed it, is now more of a town, with 4,000 inhabitants.

The growth of Kingskerswell is something of an exception to the rule that has prevailed over the past 150 years - most villages have shrunk in that time, their populations having been drawn away by

economic vicissitudes and the lure of employment in the cities and towns. Villages near to centres of population, such as Kingskerswell (and even more dramatically Ivybridge, which has grown from 500 in the 19th century to approaching 20,000 today), have thrived by becoming mere dormitories for the cities. Elsewhere the growing mechanisation of agriculture and the failure of local industry in the shape of mining, cloth milling or fishing have in some cases almost halved village populations. Morchard Bishop, for example, had a population of 1800 in 1851, but the building of a new turnpike away from the village reduced its numbers to 1000 within fifty years.

Some villages no longer exist as they appear in these photographs simply because they have been swallowed up by the cities or towns from which they were once separated by fields and woodland. Babbacombe has been engulfed by the hotels and bed-and-breakfasts of Torquay, for example, and Pilton is now part of Barnstaple. Drive through some of these places and you could be forgiven for thinking of them merely as suburbs, blissfully unaware that they were once self-sufficient communities in their own right.

In past centuries, before the arrival of the railways and particularly the advent of the car, populations were far less mobile than today. Almost everything that was needed to sustain life would have been available locally: quarries nearby would have provided building stone, reed beds or straw from the fields provided thatch; food came from the land, and beer from the pub, which very likely brewed its own; a host of craftsmen and artisans, such as wheelwrights, thatchers, carpenters, weavers, millers and bakers, provided the rest of life's necessities. Social needs were met by the inn, and spiritual ones by the church. There was little need, or indeed opportunity, to leave the village except on the occasions it was necessary to take something to market or, for some isolated souls, to go to church.

Church and pub often sit side by side on the village green, and this is no accident. The masons and carpenters who built the church needed accommodation, and a house would often be built in which they could stay, a house which would later become a pub, sometimes named the Church House Inn as at Harberton or Stokenham. Other pubs were built to allow footsore worshippers the chance of refreshment before trudging back home, for some parishes, particularly on the moor, were huge and could involve a walk of several miles to worship. Lydford parish, the largest in England, covered 88 square miles!

Even on the day of rest, then, farm workers, miners, fishermen and their families could not put their feet up. It was part of a pattern of life that took a toll on even the most hardy: hard slog from dawn to dusk, most likely poorly paid, a diet that barely met nutritional needs, and little in the way of medical care if you fell ill or were injured. Life was

cheap; the rural idyll, as portrayed in books and on film, was very different if you actually had to live it. Devonians come from hardy stock, however; they managed to survive, even thrive at times, in their little self-contained settlements, and trooped off dutifully each Sunday to give thanks for their lot.

The walls of the village church reflect the landscape in which they stand. On Dartmoor they will be built in granite, robust and plain because it is difficult to work, whereas in the east of the county the material may be the pale Beer stone, which lends itself to carving and decoration, or perhaps a red sandstone. In the south of the county cool white limestone and grey-green Dartmouth slates are common, while throughout north Devon the brown sandstone known locally as Culm is ubiquitous.

The underlying geology is responsible for more than just building stone, however - it moulds the countryside, and each landscape is a reflection of what lies beneath. Dartmoor's granite is resistant to erosion; the moor has therefore remained high, much of it over 1200 feet, and villagers here traditionally scratched a living sheepfarming on the thin, acid soils, their homes sheltering in valleys to escape the worst of the weather. The slates and sandstones of South Devon weather down to richer soils, but the land is cut by deep river valleys running down off the moor, which makes it hilly and difficult to cultivate. It is suited to rich grazing; here, farmers raised cattle, which went for sale at market towns such as Kingsbridge, or sheep, which

provided the wool which went to mills at villages like Harbertonford. The Culm Measures, which cover two-fifths of the county, produce yet another landscape: a plateau of clayish soils dotted with villages linked by the characteristic Devon lane, narrow, bendy and hemmed in on each side by high hedges.

The villages show as much variety as the landscape. Take Clovelly and Torcross, for example. Both are fishing villages, but about the only thing they have in common is that their fleets are a fraction of the size they once were and that they now rely on the summer tourist trade. Clovelly's houses cling to an improbably steep, wooded hillside, at the bottom of which crabbers and longliners shelter behind the sturdy 18th-century harbour wall. At Torcross there is no harbour; boats have to be pulled clear of the tide up the shingle bank on which the village stands, while the postman is hardly likely to give himself a hernia carrying his sack around the flat streets.

The moorland villages, in which development has been restricted because of their location within the National Park, have preserved at least the ghostly outline of what life was once like. Seen from the heights of Bonehill Rocks or Hamel Down, Widecombe-in-the-Moor looks much as it must have done in the 19th century, with only the sun glinting off the windscreen of a passing car or coach betraying the fact that this is the 21st century. Farmers still graze their sheep in the fields around

the village or on the common grazing of the open moor. However, Widecombe Fair now exists to part the tourists from their money, and no longer sees hundreds of Dartmoor ponies changing hands, while the pubs now provide pasties and sandwiches not for weary worshippers on a Sunday, but for carloads of summer visitors.

The growth of the tourist trade has brought the most profound changes to some villages. Before the building of the railways and the appearance in Edwardian times of a middle class who had both the time and money to take holidays, places like Woolacombe and Croyde were tiny, isolated farming communities. Today, although the old centre of Croyde remains, it is surrounded by vast caravan parks, campsites and holiday cottages, while Woolacombe's sea front is thick with hotels and restaurants.

Away from the tourist traps of seaside and moorland, however, and off the main roads with their convoys of cars, coaches and caravans, it is still possible to find what might be called 'working'

villages. The Culm plateau, extending north from Dartmoor to the sea, is crossed by only a few main roads, and between these red lines on the map lie large areas of terra incognita, criss-crossed with a maze of lanes on which traffic consists of tractors, Land Rovers and the odd battered pick-up with a couple of bales of hay in the back. Life here still revolves around the working of the land; the rhythm of the seasons dictates not whether the cash tills are ringing in the tea-rooms, but the age-old imperatives of milking, lambing and haymaking.

In 1086, when William the Conqueror ordered the compiling of the Domesday Book, nine out of every ten Devonians lived in the countryside, making their living from fishing or farming. Today the balance has almost completely reversed. But although the mill might now dispense cream teas, and the forge sell postcards, the church and pub will still be there, the patches of grey and gold lichen on their old building stone indicating that the passage of time does not change everything.

West Devon & Dartmoor

Lifton, The Railway Station c1900 L195501
The railway line here is the Lydford to Launceston
extension of the South Devon Line, which opened
in 1865 and ran until the 1960s. The site of the
square building in the middle distance is now
occupied by the area's largest employer, the
Ambrosia rice pudding factory, and the road on the
left is now the A30.

◄ **Endsleigh, Coombe Lodge 1908** 59734
Coombe Lodge is the gatehouse for Endsleigh Cottage (actually a considerable house), which stands in a magnificent position high on a hillside above a sharp bend in the Tamar. It was built by the Duke of Bedford in 1810.

◀ **Milton Abbot, The Church and the Village 1908** 59733
Once part of the Tavistock Abbey estates, and acquired by the Duke of Bedford during the Reformation, Milton Abbot is something of an oasis of stability in that it has only had two landowners in over a thousand years, and is largely unchanged from the way it looks in this picture. The houses were designed by Sir Edwin Lutyens.

▼ **Lydford, General View 1907** 57506
The wild open spaces of Dartmoor are still used by the army for training, but rarely can it have been used on such a vast scale as this - look at the enormous encampment spreading along the edge of the moor on what is now Willsworthy ranges.

◀ **Lydford The Dartmoor Inn 1922** 73166
Lydford has an historical importance out of all proportion to its size. The fort was first built by Alfred the Great in the time of the Danish invasions, and it was also an important Saxon Mint. A royal borough at the time of the Domesday Book, Lydford eventually lost influence with the building of Launceston Castle across the Cornish border.

▼ **Lydford, The Manor Hotel 1895** 36330

Lydford's 15th-century church of St Petroc has in its churchyard the grave of watchmaker George Routleigh, who ' ... departed this life on November 14, 1802 aged 57. Wound up in hope of being taken in hand by his Maker and of being thoroughly cleaned and repaired and set agoing in the world to come'. They don't write epitaphs like that any more.

▼ **Whitchurch, The Village 1910** 62269

This sturdy embankment, carrying the South Devon and Tavistock Line, was built by Isambard Kingdom Brunel; it opened in 1859, the same year that his famous bridge opened at Saltash. How did he find the time? The railway closed in 1968.

▲ **Whitchurch
The Village 1910** 622(

The church of St Andre was built in the 15th century, but it is though that the village takes its name from an earlier church which was built from the white elvan or quarried on nearby Roborough Down.

◄ **Horrabridge
The Church
and the Village 1898**
42242
In 1501 the bridge here over the River Walkham was crossed by none other than Katherine of Aragon, on her way to London from Plymouth to marry Arthur, eldest son of Henry VII. Arthur died within a year, and Katherine went on to marry his younger brother, Henry VIII.

**Bere Alston
The Village 1898** 42262
Although only a few miles
from Plymouth to the
south and Tavistock to the
north, Bere Alston feels
quite remote, situated
on the peninsula between
the Tamar and Tavy.
Before the arrival of the
railway, only eight years
before this picture was
taken, the sense of
isolation must have been
even greater.

▼ **Bere Ferrers, General View 1898** 42257
Situated near the tip of the peninsula, Bere Ferrers is even more
isolated than Bere Alston. It takes its name from the Ferrers family,
who acquired the manor during the rule of Henry II and built the
church of St Andrew (centre) in 1333.

▼ **Yelverton, General View 1898** 42250
Yelverton owes its existence to the railway. In 1883 the old Princetown
line was modernised and joined the Plymouth to Tavistock line at
Yelverton, which became home to the Victorian villas seen here.

▲ **Yelverton, The Corn‹
Cafe and the Green
1934** 86253
This picture is taken at
Leg O'Mutton, looking
north-east towards
Sharpitor. Wherry's Ca
is now a newsagent, ar
the Beechfield Hotel a
Cafe. It appears that e\
in 1934 Dartmoor por
had learned that touris
were a soft touch for
food!

◄ Milton Combe, Brookside Stores and Post Office c1965 M170025
Away from the moors, the cost of transporting granite was prohibitive for all save the wealthy, and so its use was limited. Here, the walls are made from the easily-split local slate, while the granite is used only for decoration. Here it caps the wall and, because of its strength, is probably used for the lintels, such as those over the wider doors on the left.

◀ **Two Bridges
The Hotel c1950**

T153003

This is an excellent spot for a well-earned pint on the lawn after a hot summer walk over the tors, or for sheltering from the elements during the winter. Two Bridges is the cross-roads of the moor, and the bridges in question - one an ancient packhorse bridge and the other a road bridge - span the West Dart River

Princetown, General View
1931 84059

Princetown is a monument to the persistence of one man - Sir Thomas Tyrwhitt. He owned quarries nearby, and was responsible for the arrival of the first (horse-drawn) railway in 1823 which supplied the prison (also built by Tyrwhitt in 1806), and which also brought much-needed home comforts such as coal for the inhabitants of this desolate spot.

Shaugh Prior
The Village c1965
S356018

The striking granite tower of the 15th-century church of St Edward, King and Martyr, sitting 700 feet above sea level on the southern fringe of the moor, is visible (on a clear day, of which Dartmoor does not get many!) from several miles out to sea.

Wotter, The Village
c1960 W277017

Wotter grew as a clay mining village. Vast workings of kaolin (china clay) on Lee Moor to the north and west have been worked since 1840. This part of Dartmoor has many Bronze Age monuments, some of which were lost in an extension of the clay pits.

◄ **South Brent, The View from Lydia Bridge c1960** S360006
This lovely, rambling old house still stands on the west bank of the Avon. In the past, builders often used stones from the bed of the river to construct houses around here. These smooth stones needed little dressing and could be used straight from the river, but are something of a headache if you need to drill holes for shelves!

◄ Harford, General View c1955 H237010

Harford sits on the east bank of the Erme, which rises at 1200 feet on the moor and reaches the sea at Mothecombe. The pretty granite church was built in the late 15th century; it is dedicated to St Petrock, a common saint in these parts and in Cornwall.

▼ Buckfastleigh The Abbey from the Parish Church c1960

B238043

Buckfast Abbey is a monument to devotion and persistence. Standing on the site of the old abbey which was destroyed in the Reformation, it was built between 1882 and 1932 by the Benedictine monks themselves.

◄ Holne, The Approach to the Village c1960

H101001

In 1743 the churchwardens of Holne approved the casting of five new bells 'for the sum of three score pounds'. St Mary's Church is 14th-century, as is the Church House Inn, a listed building with a great selection of beers.

◀ **Haytor Vale
The Village 1906** 5658
A mile west of here is
Haytor itself; it is now a
tourist honeypot, but in
the past it was an
important quarrying site
which almost certainly
provided the granite for
this terrace with its
robust chimney stacks.
The stone was carried
on a granite tramway,
which opened in 1820.

◀ **Buckland, The Village 1931** 84036
Buckland in the Moor (to give it its full name) is perhaps the archetypal Devon village: thatched granite cottages hide among the trees on a hillside above the River Webburn, approached through a maze of narrow lanes.

▼ **Haytor, The Village 1931** 83925
The building with the dark gable is the Haytor Rock Hotel, once a haunt of 'My Lady of the Moor', the romantic novelist Beatrice Chase, who died in 1955 aged eighty. Haytor was originally called Idetor, which was eventually corrupted to High Tor and then Hey Tor.

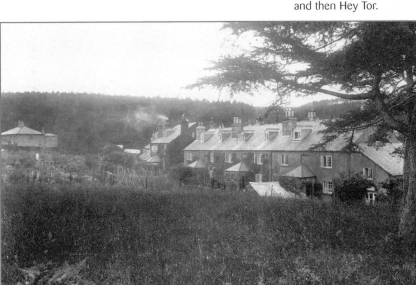

◀ **Ilsington, The Village and the Church 1940** 89051
The 14th-century church of St Michael has a small room above the lychgate, which was once used as a school room; it was the site of a strange accident in 1639. A parishioner closed the gate a little too enthusiastically and the south wall collapsed, throwing four pupils into the street and burying the other seventeen and their teacher. Remarkably, no-one was killed.

◄ **Widecombe in the Moor The Village c1960**

W95031

Go down this road and take the next turning right and you will arrive at the Rugglestone Inn. Named after a huge lump of granite on the hillside nearby, the Rugglestone is one of the moor's gems: a tiny pub with a flagged floor and a welcoming fire.

◀ Widecombe in the Moor The Old Inn 1922

73148

The characters in the song 'Widecombe Fair' are thought not to have come from Widecombe, but from twenty miles or so to the north-west. Tom Pearce was a mill owner in Sticklepath, and Tom Cobley died in Spreyton in 1794.

Lustleigh ▶ The Tudor Memorial 1924

76510

This cross has nothing to do with the family who ruled England for so long - it actually commemorates Henry Tudor, rector of the parish from 1888 to 1904. The drinking trough is nowadays filled with flowers.

◀ Lustleigh The Village c1965

L115074

The church of St John the Baptist was originally built in the 13th century, but like many churches, more parts were added through to the 16th century. An old tradition took place here on Plough Sunday, when a wooden plough was brought into the church for blessing to ensure the success of the crops.

▼ **Lustleigh, The Cleave Hotel 1920** 69629

The cleave from which the hotel takes its name was once the site of a famous ten-ton logan stone called the Nutcrackers, which in 1950 fell into the valley. 1200 man-hours were spent by a Major Graham and 40 soldiers trying to replace it, but to no avail - it was 'too tough a nut for them to crack', according to one wit.

▼ **Lustleigh, Wreyland 1906** 56595

Although only just across the Wray Brook from Lustleigh, Wreyland is in the parish of Bovey Tracey. Its most famous resident was Cecil Torr (an apt name for a Dartmoor man), author of 'Small Talk at Wreyland', a charming and fascinating amalgam of local lore and anecdotes.

▲ **Manaton, The Green 1922** 73160

Half a mile from here is Wingstone Farm, home for many years of John Galsworthy, author of 'The Forsyte Saga' and 'The Pallisers'. Galsworthy was a stalwart of the Manaton Cricket Club, but in seventeen seasons play he failed to score a single run.

◄ **North Bovey, The Church and the Lychgate 1907** 58512
The centre of North Bovey has everything a village should - a green with oak trees, the Ring O'Bells, a 13th-century thatched pub, and the church of St John, also 13th-century. The cottage dates from the 18th century, and is now a shop and post office.

North Bovey ▶
The Cross 1907 58516
This is not the original, medieval cross - that was smashed during the Civil War. The present one was found in Bovey Brook in 1829 by the Rev John Pike Jones, and was erected at the edge of the green.

▼ **Dunsford**
The Village c1960
D118015
Situated on a hilltop above the valley of the Teign (visible just left of centre in the distance), Dunsford is home to Brimblecombe's Farm Cider. To the north is Great Fulford, home of the Fulford family; theirs is the oldest family in Devon, tracing its lineage back to Richard I and the Crusades.

▲ **Drewsteignton**
The Village c1950
D85003
Round the corner on the left is the Drewe Arms, named after the Drewe family; they employed Edwin Lutyens to design the nearby Castle Drogo, now owned by the National Trust. The Drewe Arms's landlady for seventy-five years was Mabel Mudge, who retired at the age of ninety-nine having saved the pub from any modernisation.

◀ **Belstone, The Post Office c1960** B296020
Set high on the edge of the moor, in the shadow of Belstone Tor (1568 feet) and looking down on the waters of the Taw rushing through Belstone Cleave, this village was home for a while to John Trevena, author of 'Furze the Cruel', 'Heather' and 'Granite'.

South Devon

Bovisand, General View 1925 78502
For generations, Bovisand has been the favoured
venue with Plymothians for a day out on the beach.
The grassy area on which the tents stand remains
undeveloped today, but the hillside inland is now
covered with holiday chalets, which stretch almost
as far as Bovisand Point in the background.

▼ **Wembury, The Church and the Beach c1955** W604002
The 14th-century church of St Werburgh dominates this view of
Wembury Beach, which is now owned by the National Trust. Just beyond
the small rock point left of centre is the mouth of the River Yealm, the
estuary of which runs inland to Newton Ferrers and Noss Mayo.

▼ **Newton Ferrers, Bridgend 1936** 87477
It is high tide, and we are looking down the small creek which divides
Newton on the north shore from Noss Mayo on the south. In the centre
is the tower of the church of St Peter, built at Noss in 1880 by Edward
Baring (later Lord Revelstoke), a member of the well-known banking family.

▲ **Noss Mayo
The River Yealm 19.**
83981
On the right is Newton
Ferrers, considerably
smaller than it is today
Noss, however (centre
and left), remains much
the same, although the
Globe has been extend
and renamed the Ship
Both Newton and Nos
are home to pilot gigs
and crabbers which ar
raced with gusto - and
keen local rivalry - dur
the summer.

◀ **Noss Mayo**
The Village and the River
Yealm 1930 83096
On the opposite shore from the
Ship, and slightly downstream,
is the Swan (centre), which
serves a fine crab sandwich.
Small rowing boats such as the
ones here are still common, but
out on the river the moorings
are now occupied by modern
pleasure craft.

▼ Challaborough, The Bay and Burgh Island c1950 C301005

It is a wintry day, with far fewer caravans and chalets in evidence than are to be seen today. On the left of the Island is the famous art deco hotel, built in 1929, and on top of the island is a far older structure - the Huers' Hut, which was used as a lookout for the pilchard shoals that were once the main local industry.

▼ Ringmore, The Post Office c1960 R258018

Ringmore, just inland from Challaborough, was once a smugglers' haunt: legend has it that the 13th-century local pub, the Journey's End, is linked by tunnel to nearby Ayrmer Cove. The Post Office (left) has moved, and the building is now a private house called Ivy Cottage.

▲ Bantham General View 1920

69847
The Avon was once a thriving salmon river, and Bantham, at its mouth, was a busy port transhipping limestone and coal and exporting corn and potatoes. Salmon are rare now, and the coasters never visit this sheltered and beautiful estuary. The Sloop Inn was once owned by John Whiddo of 'Widecombe Fair' far

◄ **Loddiswell, The Old
School House and the
Village c1955** L531014
Loddiswell lies just east of
Aveton Gifford on the River
Avon, and is recorded as
a salmon fishery in the
Domesday Book. The raised
terrace is a feature of many
Devon villages, and is likely
these days to be full of cars.

**Thurlestone
The Village 1924**

76558

Smuggled kegs of brandy used to be stored in the top of the porch at the 13th-century church of All Saints here. The rector traditionally took one keg as payment - until in 1839 a new, strait-laced incumbent 'indignantly refused it'.

◀ **Salcombe
General View c1965**

S44219
Until the middle of the
19th century, Salcombe
was primarily a fishing
and trading port. The
arrival of the railway at
nearby Kingsbridge in
1893 boosted its growth
as a resort, and today it
is home to yachtsmen
and hotels. On the right
is the church of Holy
Trinity, built in 1843.

South Milton
The Church 1927

79893

In 1772 the 'Chantiloupe' was wrecked on South Milton Sands. A wealthy lady passenger, determined to preserve her fortune, donned all her jewellery before swimming ashore; she was found by wreckers, who cut off her fingers for her rings before realising she was still alive.

Chillington
The Village 1904   52463

At one time around the 14th century, Chillington was rather optimistically described as a borough, perhaps the result of delusions of grandeur on the part of the local squire, for it has remained a village, and an attractive one at that, located on the A379 east of Kingsbridge.

East Portlemouth
General View 1925

78398

Although only ten minutes' ferry ride across the estuary from Salcombe (background left), East Portlemouth is actually quite remote, and therefore has never undergone large-scale development. On the far horizon are the hills of South Dartmoor.

**Hallsands
Fishing Boats 1924**

76533

These robust little boats were launched straight from the beach. Start Bay faces east and is therefore sheltered from the prevailing westerlies, but winter easterlies could keep the fleet ashore. Crabs were a favourite catch, caught in pots woven from reed harvested from nearby Slapton Ley.

**Torcross
The Sands 1920** 69837
Torcross takes its name
from the high rock
which stands at the end
of the long beach,
which is known locally
as the Line. It is thought
that the rock once had
a cross on it to act as a
mark for shipping. Just
out of sight is the 15th-
century church of St
Michael and All Angels.

◄ **Slapton, Church Lane 1925** 78250
The 15th-century church of St James the Greater is not far from the ruined tower of the 14th-century Chantry, from which the nearby Tower Inn takes its name. Many of the buildings around here are built from Dartmouth slate, which splits easily to form the characteristic thin blocks seen in the house on the right.

◀ Torcross
General View 1930
83276
We are looking west across the unique, 270-acre freshwater lagoon of Slapton Ley, haunt of fishermen and bird watchers and their respective preys. At the Ley's edge are beds of Slapton reed, much sought after for thatching because of its durability.

▼ Slapton, The Royal Sands Hotel 1924 76528
This fine hotel survived everything nature could throw at it for over a hundred years, but it finally succumbed to the attentions of a disobedient dog in 1944: the hotel had been mined by the army, and both dog and building disappeared in a spectacular explosion. The site is now a car park.

◀ Strete
The Church and the School 1925 78263
When the church of St Michael was built in 1836, Strete was still part of the parish of Blackawton, which had been a royal manor from Saxon times and also had a church dedicated to St Michael. Strete was originally called Street, but it changed its name in 1870 so as to avoid confusion with the village of the same name in Somerset.

▼ **Strete, The Village 1925** 78260

Strete stands 300 feet up on a hill at the north end of the old turnpike to Torcross, now the A379 to Dartmouth. Built on the shingle bank of the Line, the road is vulnerable to the elements; as recently as January 2001 it was damaged by storms.

Stoke Fleming ▶ The Village 1925

78383

Just opposite the church of St Peter (a long-standing landmark for sailors) is the Green Dragon, a 17th-century pub, which like so many others on this coast, is reputed to have a tunnel through which smugglers brought their contraband from the beach.

▲ **Harbertonford The Bridge c1960**

H494001

Built on a crossing poir of the Harbourne River a tributary of the Dart, Harbertonford is not always the tranquil spo pictured here. In 1999 and 2000 it was floode five times in eighteen months, a series of events which must hav been a little trying for t patience of the locals a their insurers.

◀ **Duncannon**
The River Dart 1924
76472
The paddle steamer 'Compton Castle', which we can see on the left, made regular excursion trips from the Steamer Quay at Totnes (home latterly of Pete Goss's Team Phillips) down to Dartmouth, allowing passengers to enjoy the magnificent scenery of the Dart estuary.

Dittisham, The Village 1925 78372
The long estuaries of the rivers of South Devon - which are actually drowned river valleys formed when the sea level rose at the end of the last Ice Age - are very sheltered; as a result, they have their own microclimates, which allow market gardening and fruit growing to flourish. Dittisham, on the Dart, was once well-known for its plum orchards.

Dittisham, The Ferry Hotel 1925 78380
Before the motor car took over, the ferries were an essential mode of transport. The Dittisham ferry, which runs from the landing stage on the right to Greenway on the opposite shore, takes only foot passengers, but saves a twelve-mile road journey. The ferry at one time left here at 7am every morning to take boatyard workers to Dartmouth.

Kingswear
The Town and the River Bank 1925 78362
As well as providing a highway, the deep estuary of the Dart
has occasionally served another purpose - a handy, sheltered
anchorage where ship owners can lay up their ships in times
of economic difficulty. Just visible upriver are several vessels,
mothballed until the economy improves.

Ipplepen, The Square and the War Memorial c1960 127015
When writing 'The Hound of the Baskervilles', Sir Arthur Conan Doyle stayed with a friend in Ipplepen, who thoughtfully provided him with a carriage to explore the moor. The groom who drove the carriage was one Harry Baskerville.

Kingskerswell, The Mill 1910 62432
This was originally a grain mill called White Pot Mill, but it later became a tea garden; it is now a private house called Whitpot.

Kingskerswell
The Church 1910 62435
Kingskerswell was a centre of pottery and brewing in the 18th
century, but it now acts as a dormitory for Newton Abbot and
Torquay, and has grown to a population of 4,000. The church of
St Mary was built in the 14th century, possibly by the Dinham
family, who were lords of the manor.

Goodrington, The Sands 1922 73055
This half mile of sand is one of Torbay's most popular beaches. Goodrington has all but been absorbed into the urban sprawl of Paignton, but in 1922 it was still a discrete entity. Just inland from the sands is Goodrington Station, one of the halts on the steam-powered Torbay to Kingswear Line.

Cockington, The Village 1889 21539

Cockington was one of the original three parishes of Torquay. In the 19th century, when the Victorian building boom took off, the Mallocks, who were the principal landowners, showed an early example of 'nimbyism' by resisting development of the village - which explains why, even today, the village looks exactly the same as in this picture.

Babbacombe, The Beach 1925 78446

One of the steepest roads in Devon - 1 in 3 - zigzags its way down the hillside to the tiny beach at Babbacombe, which is the place where the 'English Riviera' was born. Babbacombe was hosting visits from royalty when Torquay was just a fishing village.

Shaldon, The Beach 1918 68559
Drawn up on the beach is the foot ferry, disembarking passengers from Teignmouth on the opposite shore of the Teign estuary. The prominent headland is The Ness, through which a tunnel (just visible) runs to the little beach at Ness Cove.

Shaldon, The Village 1938 88615

Shaldon is linked with Teignmouth by a road bridge, first built from wood in 1827 and now replaced by a modern steel structure. The Teign is the only one of South Devon's estuaries to have a bridge across it.

Coombe Cellars, The River 1925 78534

A couple of miles up the Teign estuary from Shaldon, and approached down a narrow lane, Coombe Cellars was once frequented by smugglers who used the pub cellar to store their contraband. Small boats still ply the river today, helmed by sailors from the yacht club rather than smugglers.

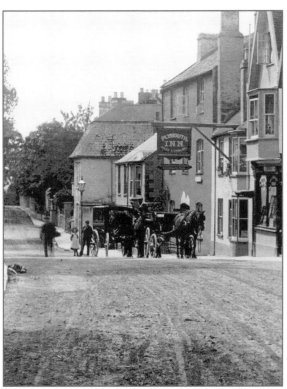

Chudleigh
Church Hill 1907 58492
Until 1550 Chudleigh was owned by the Bishops of Exeter, and was at one time a borough in its own right; but like many smaller Devon towns, it declined in the second half of the 19th century. However, it remained important as a halt for travellers (such as these stagecoaches here) until the 1970s, when the A38 was routed along the new dual carriageway to the west.

Dawlish, Looking West 1928 81169
The Great Western Railway was the making of Dawlish; it arrived in 1846, built by Brunel, and the iron bridge on the left was built in 1887 to commemorate Queen Victoria's golden jubilee. The river is Dawlish Water, which flows through the little park of The Lawn over a series of weirs.

**Dawlish Warren
Warren Halt
The Cornish Express
1907** 58118
The low spit of land
guarding the mouth of
the Exe on the right of
this picture is Dawlish
Warren, now a nature
reserve with 180
species of birds visiting
annually and 450 types
of flowering plants. The
station was built in
1912.

East Devon

Countess Wear, The Village 1906 53980
Now little more than a suburb of Exeter, Countess
Wear grew around the paper mill that was built here
in the late 17th century. The bridge, built in 1774,
was the lowest crossing of the Exe until the M5 was
built in the 1970s.

▼ **Rockbeare, The Village c1960** R257003

Not far from here is Rockbeare Manor, built by the banker and wool merchant Sir John Duntze between 1760-70. Today the village is a rather noisier place than in Sir John's time, as it is on the flightpath of Exeter Airport.

▼ **Woodbury, The School c1965** W129027

The name of the village means 'wooden fort'; this refers to the Iron Age fort to the east, which occupies a site overlooking the estuary of the Exe. Woodbury Common is used for training by Royal Marines from the nearby camp at Lympstone.

▲ **Woodbury The White Hart and the Church c19**

W129014

Why are pubs and churches often so clo together? Because the church builders had t have somewhere to s during construction, which is what they di here. The church of S Swithin dates from th 15th century, as does the pub.

Culmstock, General View c1960 C312312

R D Blackmore wrote 'Lorna Doone' at the vicarage here when his father was curate. The church of All Saints has a 250-year-old yew tree growing from the top of its tower.

◄ **Newton Poppleford
The Post Office
and the Village c1965**
N82042
A good selection of sixtie[s]
vehicles is pulled up outs[ide]
the Post Office: a Morris
Minor, the ubiquitous
Commer van, a Ford Zeph[yr]
and, coming up the hill, a[n]
A35. The signs advertise
products that, like the car[s]
have vanished from the h[igh]
street: Craven A, Capstan
and Player's cigarettes, an[d]
Ilford film. And when did
you last see a cigarette
machine on the street?

◄ Tipton St John
The Village c1950

T152501

Tipton St John lies in the valley of the River Otter which, like the Culm, rises in the shadow of Staple Hill, highest point of the Blackdowns. Here a local tradesman appears to be settling the weekly account. Is he the milkman? Butcher? Fishmonger? Who knows.

▼ Newton Poppleford
Bridgend c1965   N82032

Not far from here, at the junction of the Exeter and Exmouth roads, is the oldest toll house in Devon, built in 1753. The church of St Luke was built in 1331; it was completely rebuilt in 1897.

◄ Otterton
The Village 1925   76808

Otterton lies just inland from the east bank of the Otter estuary; it was a Saxon port. In the 16th century, a sandbar formed at the mouth of the river, and it silted up. The church is built on the site of a priory built in the 11th century by monks from Mont St Michel in Normandy.

**Otterton
The Village 1925**
76807
It seems that the present inhabitants of Otterton are a competitive lot: on Boxing Day there is a raft race on the river, in April there is a duck race, and in August a chariot race and a Donkey Derby.

◄ **Sidbury**
The Village 1906 53823

The church of St Giles is a
good example of how
churches are modified and
rebuilt over the centuries.
was built on the site of a
Saxon crypt in the early
12th century, with the tow
added a few decades later
it was reconstructed in the
15th century, and repaired
in the 17th; the tower was
demolished and rebuilt in
1845, and finally the spire
was added in 1895.

◀ **Sidbury, The Village from the Bridge c1960** S128029

The hill in the distance is the site of Sidbury Castle (Sid-burh in Anglo-Saxon, meaning the fort on the Sid), a double-ramparted Iron Age earthwork over 1300 feet long and 400 feet wide. The bridge in the foreground spans the River Sid.

▼ **Salcombe Regis The Church 1928**

81059

This churchyard contains the graves of two famous scientists: the astronomer Norman Lockyer, and Sir Ambrose Fleming, who in 1904 invented the wireless valve. The village was once owned by Alfred the Great, hence the suffix Regis.

◀ **Branscombe The Church and the Village 1898** 42439

One of the traditional industries of this corner of Devon was lace making. Now, sad to say, it is almost defunct, but it employed nearly 5,000 people in the 17th century and Queen Victoria's wedding dress was made here in Branscombe. The Norman tower of the church of St Winifred is one of the oldest in Devon.

**Colyton
North Street 1907**
58041
The ancient settlement of Colyton dates from Saxon times and stands on the bank of the River Coly, which was once home to several mills. Hamlyn's mill and tannery operates today, still run by water power. The church of St Andrew has an unusual octagonal lantern on its 15th-century tower.

Beer, St Michael's Church 1903 49602
One of the most famous sons of this fishing village in the shadow of the great chalk cliffs of Beer Head was the smuggler Jack Rattenbury; on his retirement in 1837, he published 'Memoirs of a Smuggler'. It is interesting that he received a pension of a shilling a week from Lord Rolle of nearby Bovey House.

◄ **Yarcombe, The Village c1955** Y19019
An attractive little village in the Blackdown Hills near the source of the River Yarty, Yarcombe was once owned by Sir Francis Drake. The church of St John the Baptist (obviously a common dedication round here) is 15th-century.

◄ Membury, The Church and the Schools 1902
48478

This is a place with plenty of history: a Civil War skirmish near here in 1646 killed Sir Shilston Calmady, who is now commemorated in the church of St John the Baptist; there is an Iron Age hill fort to the east; and a Roman villa has been excavated nearby.

▼ Uplyme, Church Road c1960 U7011

Uplyme stands on the River Lym, just inland from Lyme Regis and a bare half-mile from the Dorset border. In the 17th century, Sarah Andrew, grand-daughter of local landowner Solomon Andrew, was courted by Henry Fielding, who later based the character of Sophia Western in 'Tom Jones' on his ex-sweetheart.

◄ Uplyme, Rocombe Lane c1960 U7006

The Lym valley was dotted with cloth mills throughout its length from the 14th to the 18th centuries, and it is said that they provided the scarlet serge for the uniforms of Queen Elizabeth's soldiery.

**Hawkchurch
The Village 1902**
48480
This is just about as far east in Devon as it is possible to get! The name of the village has nothing to do with birds of prey - it is a corruption of Hafoc's church. Hafoc is a Saxon name, which suggests that there was a church here long before the existing church, which dates from the 12th century , and is another dedicated to St John the Baptist.

Central Devon

Newton St Cyres, The Village c1965 N83003
Newton St Cyres stands on the railway between
Crediton and Exeter, originally the North Devon
Line which opened in 1855. Once over the
watershed between the catchments of the Exe and
Taw, the line follows the valley of the Taw all the way
to Barnstaple.

▼ **Cheriton Fitzpaine, The Village c1955** C305004
The village takes its name from the Anglo-Saxon for church town and from the Fitzpaine family, who owned the manor in the 13th century. It has one of the longest thatched buildings in Devon, the 145-foot old church house, now the school.

▼ **Morchard Bishop, The Post Office c1955** M173004
Morchard Bishop stands on the old Crediton-Barnstaple turnpike, and the London Inn was a staging post for travellers to Exeter and beyond. Today it plays host to other long distance travellers - walkers on the Two Moors Way.

▲ **Halberton, The Villa**
1930 83228
Halberton stands near remains of the Grand Western Canal, an 18th century folie de grande which was intended to link Topsham and Taunton, but was only completed between Tiverton and Burlescombe. The chu of St Andrew was built the 14th century; it ha particularly fine rood screen.

◄ **Halberton**
The Village 1930 83224
Between Higher Town (on
the hill) and Lower Town
(picture No 83228) is the
village pond, which is
unusual in that it is fed by
warm springs and reputedly
never freezes.

▼ Bickleigh, The Village 1930 83230

Bickleigh's 16th-century bridge spans the River Exe, which rises thirty miles to the north-east on the hills of Exmoor. The Exe was once a major salmon fishery, with records going back to the 12th century, and as late as 1949 nearly 4,000 fish a year were being caught; but today the catch is a tiny fraction of what it once was.

▼ Chettiscombe, The Village 1930 83227

Chettiscombe lies on a tributary of the Exe just north of Tiverton. Not far away is the grand Victorian house of Knightshayes Court, built in the 1870s for local MP John Heathcote Amory.

▲ Bampton
Castle Street c1955

B379023

Bampton's wealth in p. centuries was based o wool and cattle. Times have changed, but the October Fair still sees ponies brought down from Exmoor for aucti The church of St Mich has two magnificent y trees, each thought to over 500 years old, ar encircled by stone sea

◄ **Witheridge**
The Square c1960

W574008

Witheridge stands on the high land between South Molton and Tiverton. Celia Fiennes, an intrepid 17th-century traveller and diarist who journeyed in the area, described 'a high ridge of hills which discovers a vast prospect on each side full of inclosures and lesser hills'.

◀ **Sandford, Shute c1955** S759012
The church of St Swithin dates from the 12th century. It was closed for a few years after 1125 because of two men who 'had a very great dispute in so much that one murdered the other'.

◄ Witheridge
The Square c1960

W574019

The plum-red Devon General buses were once a common sight, but with deregulation the livery has changed and services have been reduced - it would be very unusual today to see two buses in the village square.

▼ South Zeal
The Village c1960   S363026

South Zeal is a tranquil place with a fine 16th-century granite pub, the Oxenham Arms, where Charles Dickens wrote 'The Pickwick Papers'. One of the more unusual features of the pub is a monolith reputed to be over 5000 years old and round which the pub was built.

◄ North Molton
General View 1900

6319

Sitting on a hill above the River Mole, North Molton was once a mining settlement, which is remembered in the name of the pub, the Tinners' Arms Inn. The 14th-century church of All Saints has one of the best medieval pulpits in Devon.

Heasley Mill, The Village c1955 H238013
This is a rich mining area with a variety of minerals: iron was mined here in Elizabethan and Victorian times, the prolific Prince Albert's mine produced copper from 1840-80, and gold, silver and lead were also worked. The ivy-covered ruins of mine buildings still stand up the valley.

Heasley Mill, The Green c1955 H238020
On the green here is a plough, probably made in a local forge. A famous fictional local blacksmith was R D Blackmore's Tom Faggus, a retired highwayman who worked in North Molton.

North Devon

Hartland
Fore Street 1929 82868
Although a mere four miles from the busy tourist route of the A39, Hartland feels like the land time
forgot; Fore Street looks today very much as it does in this photograph, but with more up-to-date cars.

▼ **Hartland, The Square 1929** 82870

Despite its isolation, Hartland was once a royal estate, owned by Alfred the Great and William the Conqueror. A couple of miles outside the village is the church of St Nectan, almost as big as a cathedral and with a 128-foot tower used by generations of mariners as a landmark.

Clovelly, High Street 1923 75159a ▶

The only safe anchorage on the inhospitable, craggy coastline between Appledore and Boscastle, Clovelly lived precariously for centuries from the herring fishery. However, Charles Kingsley's use of the village as a location in 'Westward Ho!' alerted the new breed of holidaymaker to the charm of its steep, cobbled streets; by 1890 there were three hotels.

▲ **Clovelly Transferring the Po**
1936 87552

The end of the road fo vehicles in pre-Land Rover days was the top the village; the steepne of High Street (known Up-A-Long and Down-Long) meant that the m had to be delivered by donkeys.

◄ **Buck's Mills**
Up Along 1930 83490
The square building above
the beach is a lime kiln,
used to burn limestone
brought over from South
Wales, which was then
taken inland to treat
Devon's acid soils. The cliffs
are of culm, a mixture of
sandstone and shale which
gives rise to the thin, poor
soils of the area.

▼ Buck's Mills, Village Corner 1930 83494

Buck's Mills is really no more than one street running down a wooded valley to the sea. To the east is a remote stretch of coastline - no villages, no harbours or beaches for six miles until Westward Ho!

▼ Appledore, The Quay 1923 75146

Appledore Quay, built in 1846, still stands; but these coastal trading schooners, once the lifeblood of trading along this coast, are now only memories, superseded by motor transport. Appledore has a long history of shipbuilding, and its covered shipyard was the largest in Europe when it was opened in 1970.

▲ Northam From The Golf Links 1919 69349

The tower of the church of St Margaret has long been used as a mark by sailors entering the Torridge estuary over the infamous Bideford Bar that guards the entrance. To the west is Westward Ho!, the only village in the land to have an exclamation mark in its name.

◄ **Weare Giffard
The Village
and the River 1923** 75116
Set on the banks of the
River Torridge, Weare
Giffard was in Domesday
times an important salmon
fishery; it later made its
living from strawberry
growing and boatbuilding.
In the late 18th century it
was planned to drive a canal
from here all the way to
Okehampton - something
of an undertaking in view
of the terrain. It is not
surprising that this project
never took off.

▼ Weare Giffard, The Church and the Village 1923 75117
This lovely manor house was built by the Fortescue family when they acquired the estate in 1454. The ivied building to the right is the gatehouse. Behind is the 14th-century church of the Holy Trinity.

▼ Taddiport, The Village 1923 75109
Taddiport's 17th-century bridge spans the River Torridge a couple of miles south of Torrington. The hay on the wagon may well have been winter feed for some of the area's famous North Devon cattle, a handsome breed also known as Ruby Reds.

▲ Taddiport, The Villa
1923 75113
Taddiport grew up aro
a 14th-century leper
hospital, and the chap
of St Mary Magdalene
stands. The village was
the route for clay from
the works at
Petersmarland until 18
when a railway was bu
and took the load off t
bridge.

◄ **Instow**
General View c1955
I14001
We are looking across the broad mouth of the Torridge towards Appledore, which now has no trading schooners in sight. The ship off the point is probably a coaster outbound from Bideford, which lies three miles back up the river to the left.

◄ **Pilton, The Village c1965** P52001
Pilton was one of the original boroughs of Devon under King Alfred, but it has now been engulfed by Barnstaple next door. It is home to Devon's youngest brewery, Barum's, who set up shop at the Reform Inn in 1996.

Umberleigh
The Village c1950
U27006

Umberleigh lies in the valley of the River Taw, and is the setting for Henry Williamson's 'Salar the Salmon'. The Taw drains a huge area, and is prone to burst its banks - notably in the winter of 2000, when Umberleigh was flooded three times.

▼ Landkey, View from
The East c1950 L193014

Landkey is thought to take its name from St Kea, a Celtic saint from Glastonbury who was doing missionary work among the (then) heathens of Devon in the 6th century. The church, oddly, is dedicated not to St Kea but St Paul. Just up the road, Filleigh takes its name from Fili, Kea's travelling companion.

◄ Swimbridge
General View c1955
S241007

The vicar here from 1833-79 was one Jack Russell, the 'hunting parson'; apart from riding enthusiastically to hounds, he did a spot of dog breeding on the side, creating the pugnacious little terriers that still carry his name - as does the local pub.

▼ Swimbridge, The Village c1955 S241003

Swimbridge was on the important trading route between South Molton and Barnstaple, and a bridge is recorded here in the Domesday book. Travel did not improve much for several centuries: one traveller in the 16th century described Devon roads as ' ... cumbersome and uneven, amongst rocks and stones, painful for man and horse'.

▼ Shirwell, The Village c1955 S357024

Yachtsman Sir Francis Chichester was born here in 1901. His father was rector of St Peter's, and father and son are buried in the churchyard - one on each side of the porch. Nearby is Youlston Park, the original home of the Chichesters.

▲ Croyde, The Village 1912 64544

Croyde takes its name from a Viking named Crydda who landed he over a thousand years ago, an event which is still commemorated in the Viking festival held annually in June. Just down the road is the Thatched Barn Inn, a 16th-century building which became a pub in 1978.

◀ **Georgeham**
The Village c1955 G323004
Georgeham was once the centre of a large parish which included Croyde, North Buckland, Hole and Pickwell. Named in the Domesday Book merely as ham (Anglo Saxon for village or estate), it took on its present name when the church was dedicated to St George.

▼ **Georgeham, The Village c1955** G323005
Georgeham was home to Henry Williamson, author of 'Tarka the Otter', who lived in Skirr Cottage and worked in a timber hut at Ox Cross. He died in 1980 and is buried in St George's churchyard.

▼ **Woolacombe, The Bathing Beach 1911** 63935
At the time of this photograph, the tourist industry was still in its infancy; Edwardian morals dictated the use of bathing machines, here seen lined up at the water's edge. Today such modesty is long gone, and Woolacombe, along with Putsborough and Croyde to the south, attracts thousands of surfers.

▲ **Woolacombe Watersmeet and Mor Point 1935** 87079
Morte Point, composed of razor-sharp Morte slates and swept by strong tides, is a noted ships' graveyard, and in the winter of 1852 alon five ships were lost her Just round the corner a Bull Point a lighthouse now stands to prevent such tragedies.

◄ **Mortehoe, General View 1935** 87090
The 14th-century church (St Mary) was founded by a priest named William de Tracey, and has a fine modern mosaic made by craftsmen who worked on St Paul's Cathedral. It was designed by an Oxford professor of art, aptly named Selwyn Image.

◀ **Berrynarbor
The Village c1960**
B73019
The church of St Peter
here has an arcade made
of Beer stone, quarried
on the other side of the
county. It is an indication
of the wealth of the Berry
family that they were able
to ship the stone round
Lands End, a journey of
some 240 miles.

◄ **Hele**
From Hillsborough
1923 74953
The village of Hele, just up the valley, has a watermill that dates back as far as 1525. It has been restored, and the 18-foot diameter wheel once again grinds flour. The road snaking along the clifftop is the A399 to Combe Martin.

▼ **Woody Bay**
From The West 1908
61088
It takes twenty minutes to walk down the path to Woody Bay - and considerably longer to walk back up again! To the east runs some of Devon's most spectacular cliff scenery, with the prominent, pointed prow of Castle Rock visible just above the horizon.

◄ **Parracombe**
The Village Street
c1950 P11027
Parracombe claims to be the birthplace of Christianity in Devon, with a church founded by St Petrock in the 6th century. No trace of Petrock's building remains, but the village does have two churches, one Victorian and one 16th-century.

Parracombe, The Old Post Office c1950 P11026

Parracombe's old church is only occasionally used now; it has a perfect, unspoilt Georgian interior. It was the subject in 1878 of a national protest, led by the critic John Ruskin, against its demolition.

Lynton, Old Maid's Cottage 1911 63927

Lynton is perched at the top of a 1-in-4 hill that leads down to Lynmouth. Lynmouth can also be reached by a spectacular cliff railway which drops 500 feet: two opposing carriages are pulled up through the weight of 700 gallons of water in its tank. It was built by publisher Sir George Newens in 1890.

Lynmouth
Cherry Bridge 1907 59423
Lynmouth was 'discovered' in 1812 by Percy Bysshe Shelley, who
stayed here with Harriet Westbrook, his first wife. They spent nine
weeks here and spread word of its beauty among other poets such
as Wordsworth, Coleridge and Southey, who described Lynmouth
as 'the finest spot ... that I ever saw'.

Lynmouth
Countisbury Hill 1929 82198
The A39 rises steeply out of the valley to Countisbury Common, whose
western cliffs are said, at 991 feet, to be the highest in England. Hidden
in the bend of the cliffs is the secluded little beach of Sillery Sands.

Brendon, The Village 1911 63861
Brendon (named after the Irish St Brendan) stands in the valley of the East Lyn River. Four miles south, over Brendon and Hoccombe Commons, is Doone Valley, on which it is thought R D Blackmore modelled the outlaws' hideout in 'Lorna Doone'.

Malmsmead, Lorna Doone's Farm c1960 M14059
The Doones are figures of 17th-century legend, brought vividly to life by Blackmore, who was sufficiently vague in his geographical descriptions to allow plenty of places on Exmoor to associate themselves with the outlaw family - now a staple of the tourist trade.

Malmsmead, The Ford
Lorna Doone's Farm c1960 M14023
Badgworthy Water, on which Malmsmead stands, marks the
boundary between Devon and Somerset, so this bus is presumably
in neither county. Further up the valley is the Blackmore memorial,
and south again the Doone Valley.

Index

Frith Book Co Titles

www.frithbook.co.uk

The Frith Book Company publishes over 100 new titles each year. A selection of those currently available are listed below. For latest catalogue please contact Frith Book Co.

Town Books 96pages, approx 100 photos. County and Themed Books 128pages, approx 150 photos (unless specified). All titles hardback laminated case and jacket except those indicated pb (paperback)

Title	ISBN	Price
Ancient Monuments & Stone Circles	1-85937-143-4	£17.99
Aylesbury (pb)	1-85937-227-9	£9.99
Bakewell (pb)	1-85937-113-2	£9.99
Barnstaple (pb)	1-85937-300-3	£9.99
Bath (pb)	1-85937-419-0	£9.99
Bedford (pb)	1-85937-205-8	£9.99
Berkshire (pb)	1-85937-191-4	£9.99
Berkshire Churches	1-85937-170-1	£17.99
Bognor Regis (pb)	1-85937-431-x	£9.99
Bournemouth	1-85937-067-5	£12.99
Bradford (pb)	1-85937-204-x	£9.99
Brighton & Hove (pb)	1-85937-192-2	£8.99
Bristol (pb)	1-85937-264-3	£9.99
British Life A Century Ago (pb)	1-85937-213-9	£9.99
Buckinghamshire (pb)	1-85937-200-7	£9.99
Camberley (pb)	1-85937-222-8	£9.99
Cambridge (pb)	1-85937-422-0	£9.99
Cambridgeshire (pb)	1-85937-420-4	£9.99
Canals & Waterways (pb)	1-85937-291-0	£9.99
Cardiff (pb)	1-85937-093-4	£9.99
Carmarthenshire	1-85937-216-3	£14.99
Cheltenham (pb)	1-85937-095-0	£9.99
Cheshire (pb)	1-85937-271-6	£9.99
Chester	1-85937-090-x	£12.99
Chesterfield	1-85937-071-3	£12.99
Chichester (pb)	1-85937-228-7	£9.99
Colchester (pb)	1-85937-188-4	£8.99
Cornish Coast	1-85937-163-9	£14.99
Cornwall (pb)	1-85937-229-5	£9.99
Cornwall Living Memories	1-85937-248-1	£14.99
Cotswolds (pb)	1-85937-230-9	£9.99
Cotswolds Living Memories	1-85937-255-4	£14.99
County Durham	1-85937-123-x	£14.99
Cumbria	1-85937-101-9	£14.99
Dartmoor	1-85937-145-0	£14.99
Derbyshire (pb)	1-85937-196-5	£9.99
Devon (pb)	1-85937-297-x	£9.99
Dorset (pb)	1-85937-269-4	£9.99
Dorset Coast (pb)	1-85937-299-6	£9.99
Dorset Living Memories	1-85937-210-4	£14.99
Dorset Churches	1-85937-172-8	£17.99
Down the Severn	1-85937-118-3	£14.99
Down the Thames (pb)	1-85937-278-3	£9.99
Dublin (pb)	1-85937-231-7	£9.99
East Anglia (pb)	1-85937-265-1	£9.99
East London	1-85937-080-2	£14.99
East Sussex	1-85937-130-2	£14.99
Eastbourne	1-85937-061-6	£12.99
Edinburgh (pb)	1-85937-193-0	£8.99
English Castles (pb)	1-85937-434-4	£9.99
English Country Houses	1-85937-161-2	£17.99
Exeter	1-85937-126-4	£12.99
Exmoor	1-85937-132-9	£14.99
Falmouth	1-85937-066-7	£12.99
Folkestone (pb)	1-85937-124-8	£9.99
Glasgow (pb)	1-85937-190-6	£9.99
Gloucestershire	1-85937-102-7	£14.99
Greater Manchester (pb)	1-85937-266-x	£9.99
Harrogate	1-85937-112-4	£12.99
Hastings & Bexhill (pb)	1-85937-131-0	£9.99
Heart of Lancashire (pb)	1-85937-197-3	£9.99
Helston (pb)	1-85937-214-7	£9.99
Hereford (pb)	1-85937-175-2	£9.99
Herefordshire	1-85937-174-4	£14.99
Humberside	1-85937-215-5	£14.99
Hythe, Romney Marsh & Ashford	1-85937-256-2	£9.99
Around Ipswich (pb)	1-85937-424-7	£9.99
Ireland (pb)	1-85937-181-7	£9.99
Isles of Scilly	1-85937-136-1	£14.99
Kent (pb)	1-85937-189-2	£9.99
Kent Living Memories	1-85937-125-6	£14.99
Lake District (pb)	1-85937-275-9	£9.99
Lancaster, Morecambe & Heysham (pb)	1-85937-233-3	£9.99
Leeds (pb)	1-85937-202-3	£9.99
Leicester	1-85937-073-x	£12.99
Leicestershire (pb)	1-85937-185-x	£9.99
Lincolnshire (pb)	1-85937-433-6	£9.99
Liverpool & Merseyside (pb)	1-85937-234-1	£9.99
London (pb)	1-85937-183-3	£9.99
Ludlow (pb)	1-85937-176-0	£9.99
Luton (pb)	1-85937-235-x	£9.99
Manchester (pb)	1-85937-198-1	£9.99

Available from your local bookshop or from the publisher

Frith Book Co Titles (continued)

Title	ISBN	Price	Title	ISBN	Price
New Forest	1-85937-128-0	£14.99	Suffolk (pb)	1-85937-221-x	£9.99
Newport, Wales (pb)	1-85937-258-9	£9.99	Suffolk Coast	1-85937-259-7	£14.99
Newquay (pb)	1-85937-421-2	£9.99	Surrey (pb)	1-85937-240-6	£9.99
Norfolk (pb)	1-85937-195-7	£9.99	Sussex (pb)	1-85937-184-1	£9.99
Norfolk Living Memories	1-85937-217-1	£14.99	Swansea (pb)	1-85937-167-1	£9.99
Northamptonshire	1-85937-150-7	£14.99	Tees Valley & Cleveland	1-85937-211-2	£14.99
Northumberland Tyne & Wear (pb)	1-85937-281-3	£9.99	Thanet (pb)	1-85937-116-7	£9.99
North Devon Coast	1-85937-146-9	£14.99	Tiverton (pb)	1-85937-178-7	£9.99
North Devon Living Memories	1-85937-261-9	£14.99	Torbay	1-85937-063-2	£12.99
North Yorkshire (pb)	1-85937-236-8	£9.99	Truro	1-85937-147-7	£12.99
North Wales (pb)	1-85937-298-8	£9.99	Victorian & Edwardian Devon	1-85937-253-8	£14.99
Norwich (pb)	1-85937-194-9	£8.99	Victorian & Edwardian Kent	1-85937-149-3	£14.99
Nottingham (pb)	1-85937-324-0	£9.99	Vic & Ed Maritime Album	1-85937-144-2	£17.99
Nottinghamshire (pb)	1-85937-187-6	£9.99	Victorian and Edwardian Cornwall	1-85937-252-x	£14.99
Peterborough (pb)	1-85937-219-8	£9.99	Victorian and Edwardian Sussex	1-85937-157-4	£14.99
Peak District	1-85937-100-0	£14.99	Victorian & Edwardian Yorkshire	1-85937-154-x	£14.99
Peak District (pb)	1-85937-280-5	£9.99	Victorian Seaside	1-85937-159-0	£17.99
Penzance	1-85937-069-1	£12.99	Villages of Devon (pb)	1-85937-293-7	£9.99
Piers	1-85937-237-6	£17.99	Warwickshire (pb)	1-85937-203-1	£9.99
Plymouth	1-85937-119-1	£12.99	Welsh Castles (pb)	1-85937-322-4	£9.99
Preston (pb)	1-85937-212-0	£9.99	West Midlands	1-85937-109-4	£14.99
Reading (pb)	1-85937-238-4	£9.99	West Midlands (pb)	1-85937-289-9	£9.99
Salisbury (pb)	1-85937-239-2	£9.99	West Sussex	1-85937-148-5	£14.99
St Ives	1-85937-068-3	£12.99	West Yorkshire (pb)	1-85937-201-5	£9.99
Scotland (pb)	1-85937-182-5	£9.99	Weymouth (pb)	1-85937-209-0	£9.99
Scottish Castles (pb)	1-85937-323-2	£9.99	Wiltshire Living Memories	1-85937-245-7	£14.99
Sheffield, South Yorks (pb)	1-85937-267-8	£9.99	Wiltshire (pb)	1-85937-277-5	£9.99
Somerset	1-85937-153-1	£14.99	Wiltshire Churches (pb)	1-85937-171-x	£9.99
South Hams	1-85937-220-1	£14.99	Winchester (pb)	1-85937-428-x	£9.99
Southampton (pb)	1-85937-427-1	£9.99	Windmills & Watermills	1-85937-242-2	£17.99
Southport (pb)	1-85937-425-5	£9.99	Worcestershire	1-85937-152-3	£14.99
South Devon Coast	1-85937-107-8	£14.99	York (pb)	1-85937-199-x	£9.99
South Devon Living Memories	1-85937-168-x	£14.99	Yorkshire (pb)	1-85937-186-8	£9.99
Stratford upon Avon	1-85937-098-5	£12.99	Yorkshire Living Memories	1-85937-166-3	£14.99

Frith Book Co titles available Soon

Title		ISBN	Price	Title		ISBN	Price
Canterbury Cathedral (pb)	Jul 01	1-85937-179-5	£9.99	Poole & Sandbanks (pb)	Jul 01	1-85937-251-1	£9.99
Churches of Hampshire (pb)	Jul 01	1-85937-207-4	£9.99	Shropshire (pb)	Jul 01	1-85937-326-7	£9.99
Isle of Wight (pb)	Jul 01	1-85937-429-8	£9.99	Shrewsbury (pb)	Jul 01	1-85937-325-9	£9.99
Isle of Wight Living Memories				Villages of Sussex (pb)	Jul 01	1-85937-295-3	£9.99
	Jul 01	1-85937-304-6	£14.99				
Lighthouses	Jul 01	1-85937-257-0	£17.99	1880's England	Sep 01	1-85937-331-3	£17.99

See Frith books on the internet www.frithbook.co.uk

FRITH PRODUCTS & SERVICES

Francis Frith would doubtless be pleased to know that the pioneering publishing venture he started in 1860 still continues today. A hundred and forty years later, The Francis Frith Collection continues in the same innovative tradition and is now one of the foremost publishers of vintage photographs in the world. Some of the current activities include:

Interior Decoration

Today Frith's photographs can be seen framed and as giant wall murals in thousands of pubs, restaurants, hotels, banks, retail stores and other public buildings throughout the country. In every case they enhance the unique local atmosphere of the places they depict and provide reminders of gentler days in an increasingly busy and frenetic world.

Product Promotions

Frith products are used by many major companies to promote the sales of their own products or to reinforce their own history and heritage. Frith promotions have been used by Hovis bread, Courage beers, Scots Porage Oats, Colman's mustard, Cadbury's foods, Mellow Birds coffee, Dunhill pipe tobacco, Guinness, and Bulmer's Cider.

Genealogy and Family History

As the interest in family history and roots grows world-wide, more and more people are turning to Frith's photographs of Great Britain for images of the towns, villages and streets where their ancestors lived; and, of course, photographs of the churches and chapels where their ancestors were christened, married and buried are an essential part of every genealogy tree and family album.

Frith Products

All Frith photographs are available Framed or just as Mounted Prints and Posters (size 23 x 16 inches). These may be ordered from the address below. From time to time other products - Address Books, Calendars, Table Mats, etc - are available.

The Internet

Already twenty thousand Frith photographs can be viewed and purchased on the internet. By the end of the year 2001 some 60,000 Frith photographs will be available on the internet. The number of sites is constantly expanding, each focussing on different products and services from the Collection.
The main Frith sites are listed below.
www.francisfrith.co.uk
www.frithbook.co.uk

See the complete list of Frith Books at:
www.frithbook.co.uk
This web site is regularly updated with the latest list of publications from the Frith Book Company. If you wish to buy books relating to another part of the country that your local bookshop does not stock, you may purchase on-line.

For further information, trade, or author enquiries please contact us at the address below:
The Francis Frith Collection, Frith's Barn, Teffont, Salisbury, Wiltshire, England SP3 5QP.
Tel: +44 (0)1722 716 376 Fax: +44 (0)1722 716 881 Email: sales@francisfrith.co.uk

See Frith books on the internet www.frithbook.co.uk

TO RECEIVE YOUR FREE MOUNTED PRINT

Mounted Print
Overall size 14 x 11 inches

Cut out this Voucher and return it with your remittance for £1.50 to cover postage and handling, to UK addresses. For overseas addresses please include £4.00 post and handling. Choose any photograph included in this book. Your SEPIA print will be A4 in size, and mounted in a cream mount with burgundy rule line, overall size 14 x 11 inches.

Order additional Mounted Prints at HALF PRICE (only £7.49 each*)

If there are further pictures you would like to order, possibly as gifts for friends and family, purchase them at half price (no additional postage and handling required).

Have your Mounted Prints framed*

For an additional £14.95 per print you can have your chosen Mounted Print framed in an elegant polished wood and gilt moulding, overall size 16 x 13 inches (no additional postage and handling required).

---

* IMPORTANT!
These special prices are only available if ordered using the original voucher on this page (no copies permitted) and at the same time as your free Mounted Print, for delivery to the same address

---

Frith Collectors' Guild

From time to time we publish a magazine of news and stories about Frith photographs and further special offers of Frith products. If you would like 12 months FREE membership, please return this form.

Send completed forms to:

The Francis Frith Collection, Frith's Barn, Teffont, Salisbury, Wiltshire SP3 5QP

Voucher for FREE and Reduced Price Frith Prints

Picture no.	Page number	Qty	Mounted @ £7.49	Framed + £14.95	Total Cost
		1	**Free of charge***	£	£
			£7.49	£	£
			£7.49	£	£
			£7.49	£	£
			£7.49	£	£
			£7.49	£	£

Please allow 28 days for delivery	*** Post & handling**	**£1.50**
Book Title	**Total Order Cost**	**£**

Please do not photocopy this voucher. Only the original is valid, so please cut it out and return it to us.

I enclose a sterling cheque / postal order for £ . . . . made payable to 'The Francis Frith Collection'
OR please debit my Mastercard / Visa / Switch / Amex card *(credit cards please on all overseas orders)*

Number . . . .

Issue No(Switch only) . . . . .Valid from (Amex/Switch) . . . .

Expires . . . . Signature . . . .

Name Mr/Mrs/Ms . . . .

Address . . . .

. . . .

. . . . Postcode . . . .

Daytime Tel No . . . .   Valid to 31/12/02

The Francis Frith Collectors' Guild

Please enrol me as a member for 12 months free of charge.

Name Mr/Mrs/Ms . . . .

Address . . . .

. . . .

. . . .

. . . . Postcode . . . .

Would you like to find out more about Francis Frith?

We have recently recruited some entertaining speakers who are happy to visit local groups, clubs and societies to give an illustrated talk documenting Frith's travels and photographs. If you are a member of such a group and are interested in hosting a presentation, we would love to hear from you.

Our speakers bring with them a small selection of our local town and county books, together with sample prints. They are happy to take orders. A small proportion of the order value is donated to the group who have hosted the presentation. The talks are therefore an excellent way of fundraising for small groups and societies.

Can you help us with information about any of the Frith photographs in this book?

We are gradually compiling an historical record for each of the photographs in the Frith archive. It is always fascinating to find out the names of the people shown in the pictures, as well as insights into the shops, buildings and other features depicted.

If you recognize anyone in the photographs in this book, or if you have information not already included in the author's caption, do let us know. We would love to hear from you, and will try to publish it in future books or articles.

Our production team

Frith books are produced by a small dedicated team at offices in the converted Grade II listed 18th-century barn at Teffont near Salisbury, illustrated above. Most have worked with the Frith Collection for many years. All have in common one quality: they have a passion for the Frith Collection. The team is constantly expanding, but currently includes:

Jason Buck, John Buck, Heather Crisp, Isobel Hall, Rob Hames, Hazel Heaton, Peter Horne, James Kinnear, Tina Leary, Eliza Sackett, Terence Sackett, Sandra Sanger, Shelley Tolcher, Susanna Walker, Clive Wathen and Jenny Wathen.